Author & photographer: Thierry Hebbelinck

© 2020 Thierry Hebbelinck

Self-publishing: "Galerie Hotel Saint-Michel".

All rights reserved:

This book or any portion thereof
may not be reproduced or used in any manner whatsoever
without the express written permission of the author may be
reproduced, distributed, or transmitted in any form or by any means,
including photocopying, recording, or other electronic or mechanical
methods, without the prior written permission.

Thierry Hebbelinck is a member of Sabam:

Sabam is a Belgian association of authors
composers and publishers.

Photo book southwest coast Tenerife.
(Vertical format).

The Canaries are one of the most interesting tourist destinations for Northern & Western Europeans in wintertime. Always springtime. Especially the south of Gran Canaria & Tenerife.
This coffee heavy image book shows photos of the touristic southwest beach district of Tenerife: Arona, Santa Cruz de Tenerife, island of Spain.

Photos taken during a walk of 2,1km (1,3miles) from Playa de Las Américas to Playa Los Cristianos.
Photo shoot beaches:
Playa Las Américas, Playa Del Camison, Playa Las Vistas, Playa Los Cristianos and Montaña Chayofita.
- Costa La Caleta de Adeje, Santa Cruz de Tenerife, Spain 8,4km (5 miles) from Playa Las Américas.

Vertical shots made with a full frame Dslr camera and a 45mm prime lens.
All the photos were shot during a walk, like a tourist would leave the hotel to make an afternoon walk.
Adeje photo shoot : taxi transfer from Playa Las Américas to Adeje.

Photographer: Thierry Hebbelinck

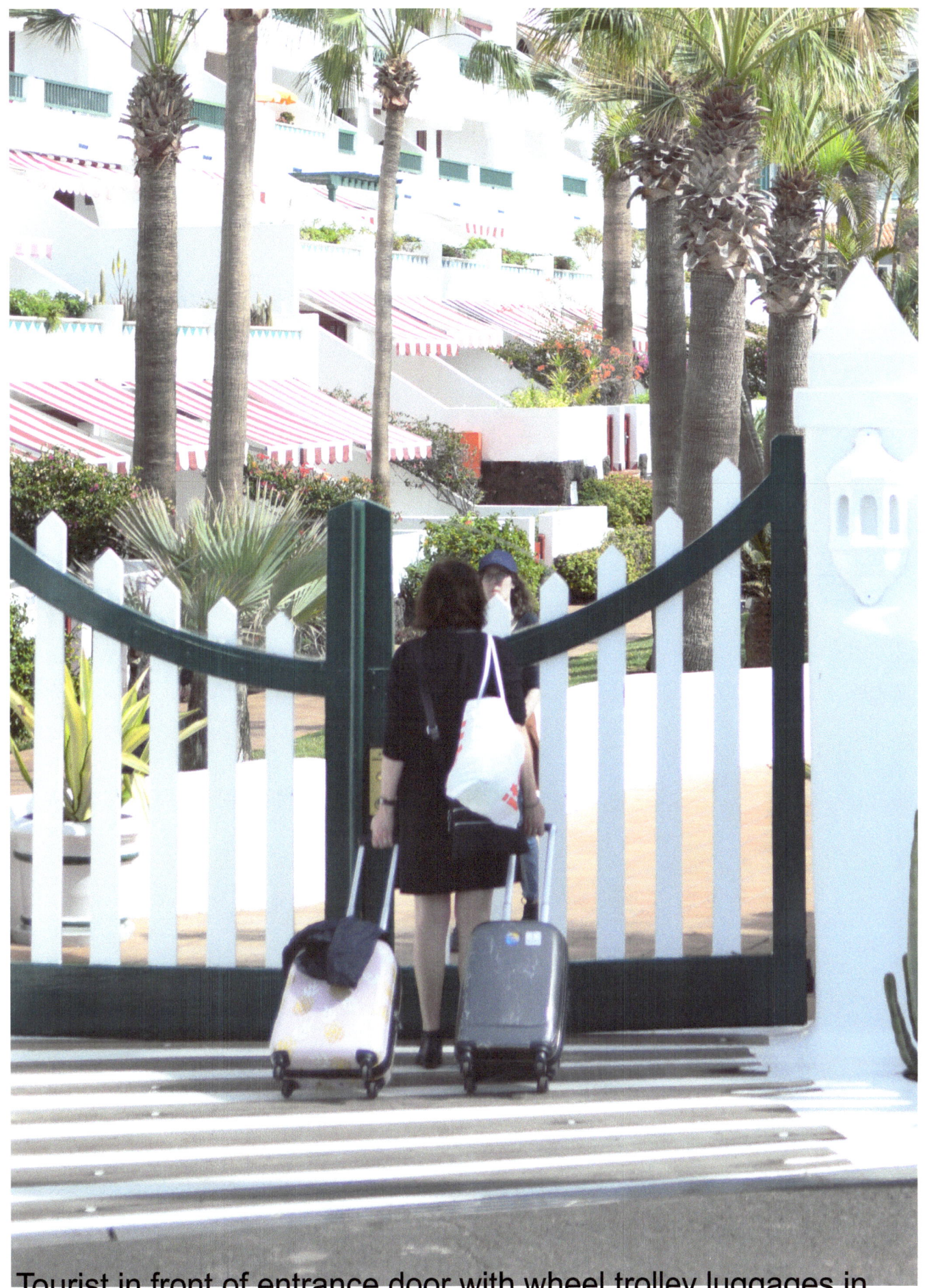

Tourist in front of entrance door with wheel trolley luggages in hands.

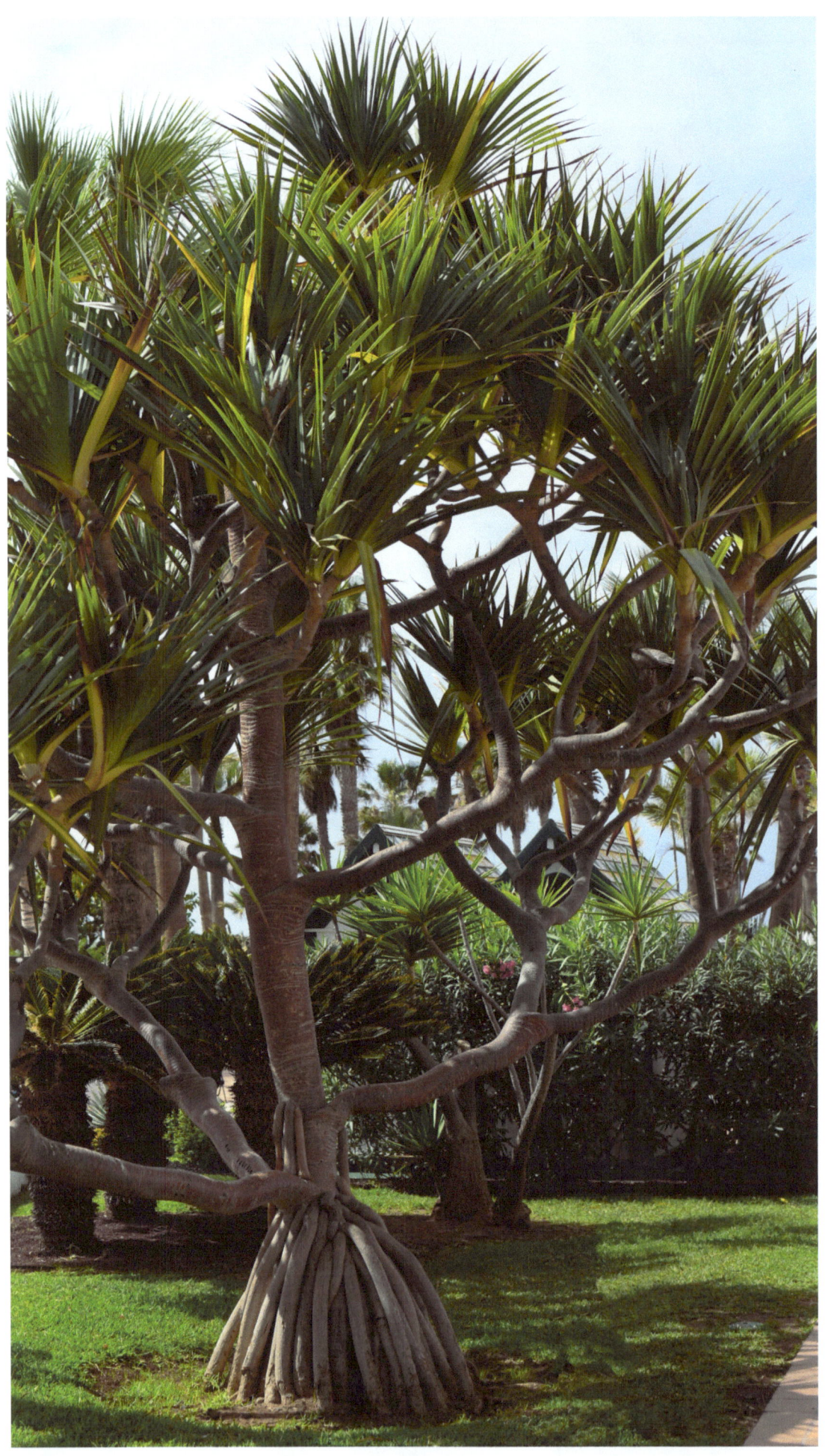

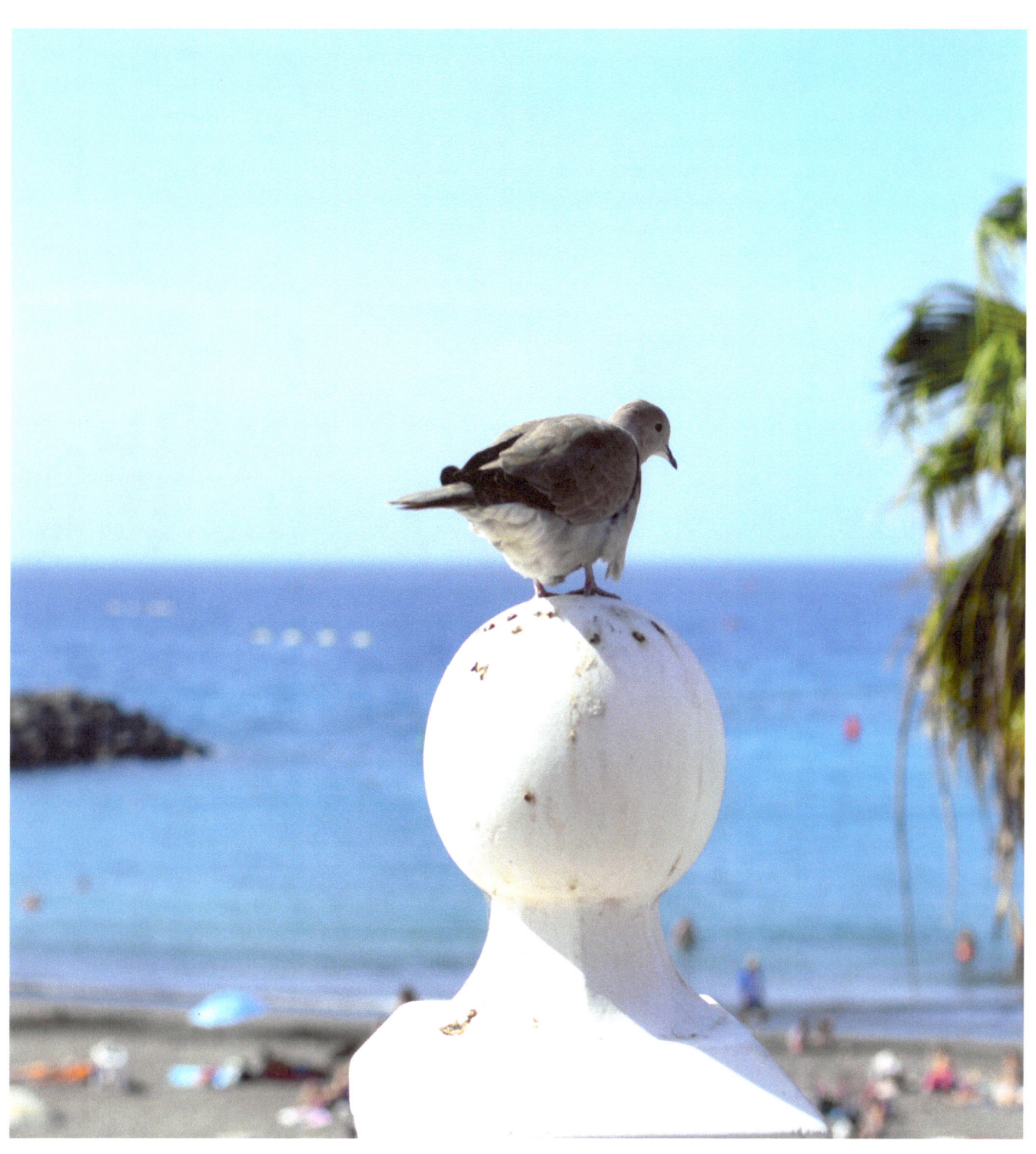

Playa Costa Adeje, Tenerife

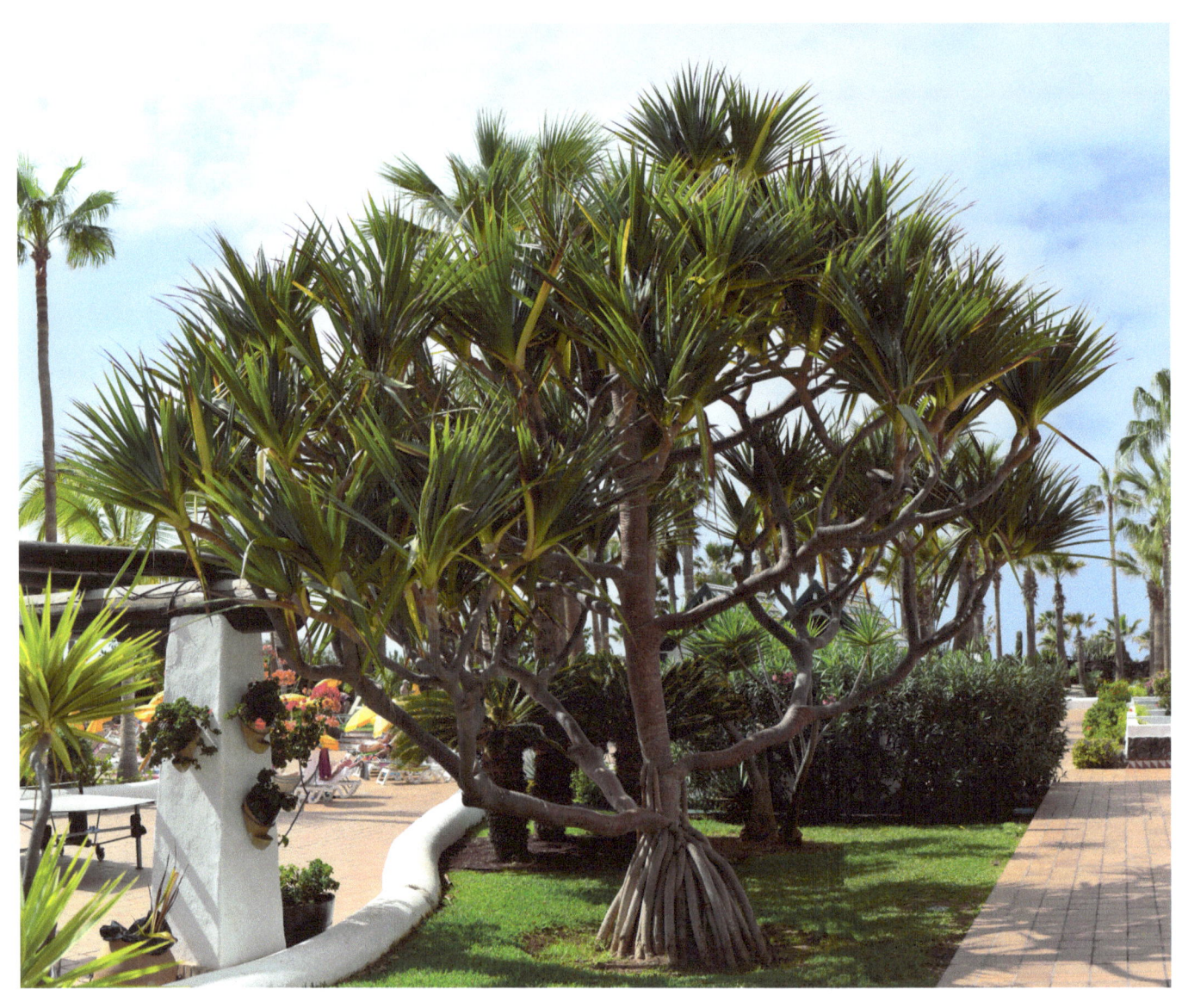

Screw pine above ground roots in Playa de Las Américas

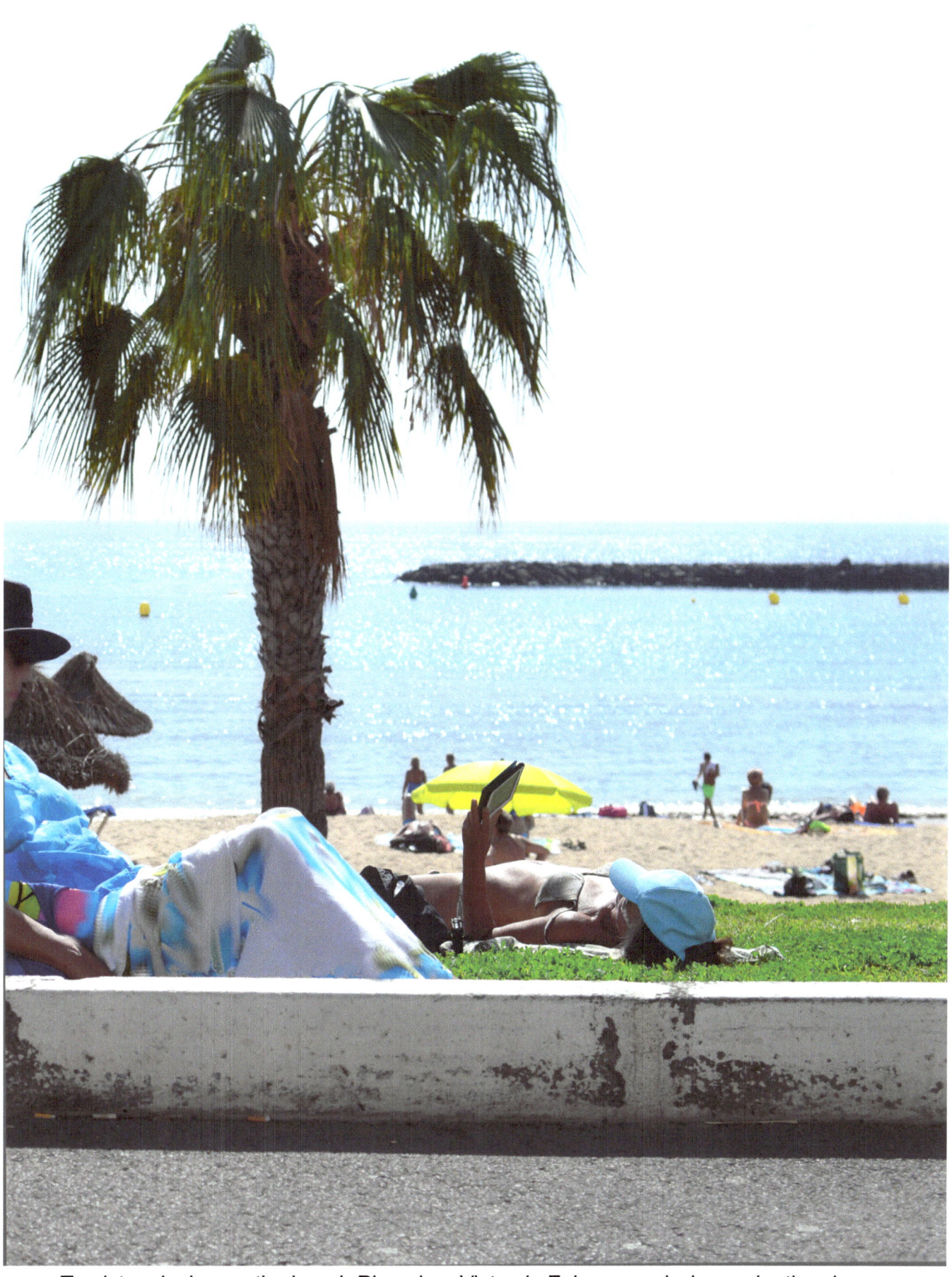

Tourists relaxing on the beach Playa Las Vistas in February enjoying springtime in a mediterranean climate of the Spanish Islands.

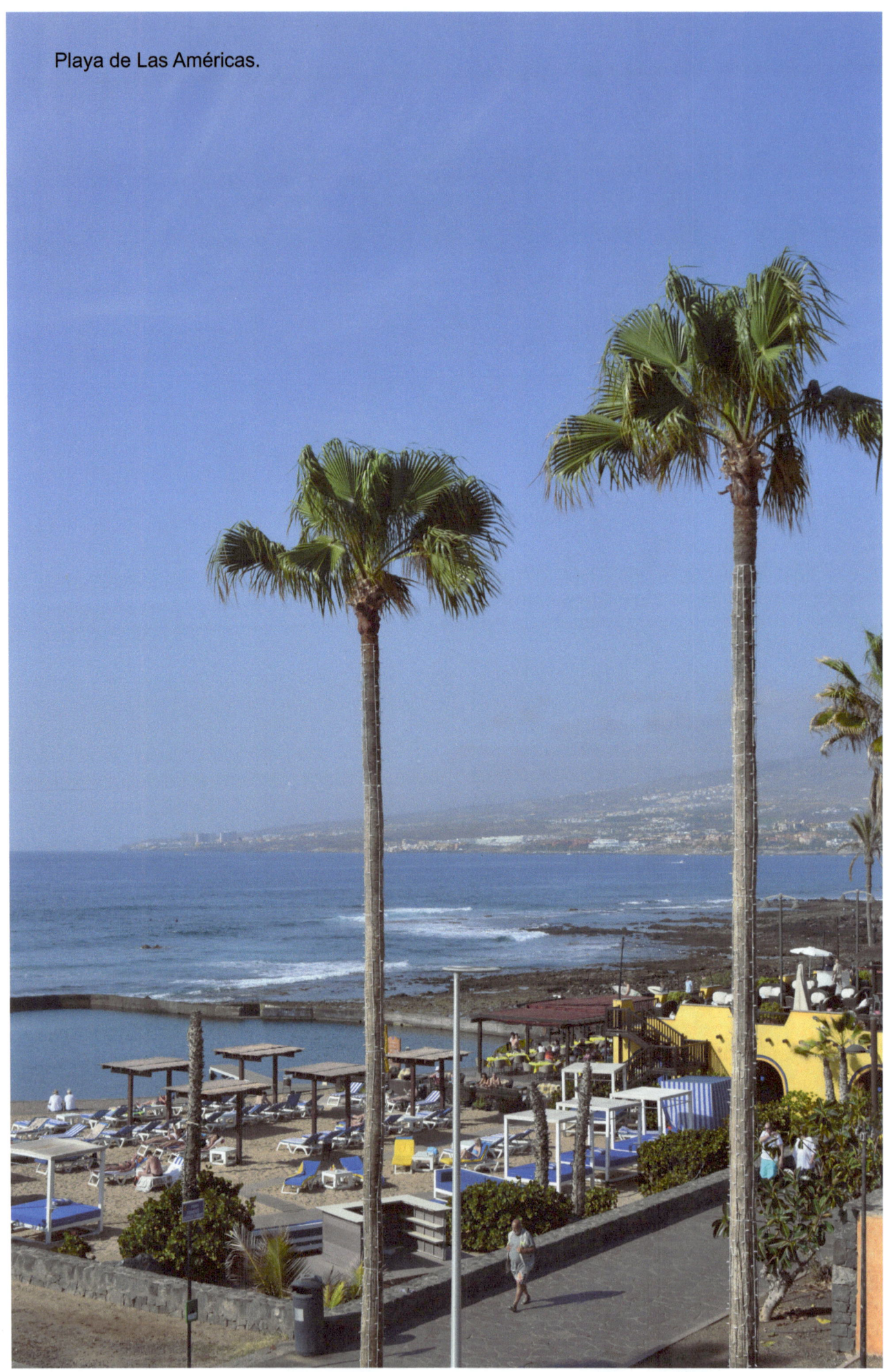

Playa de Las Américas.

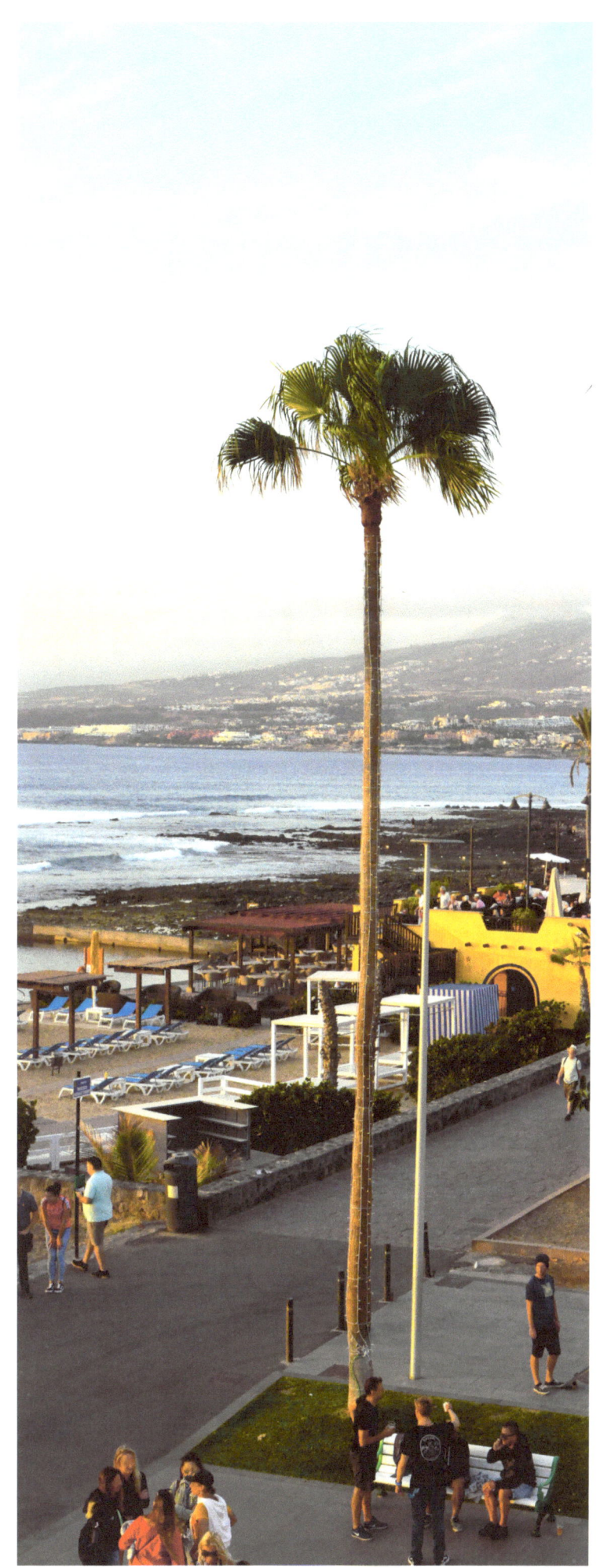

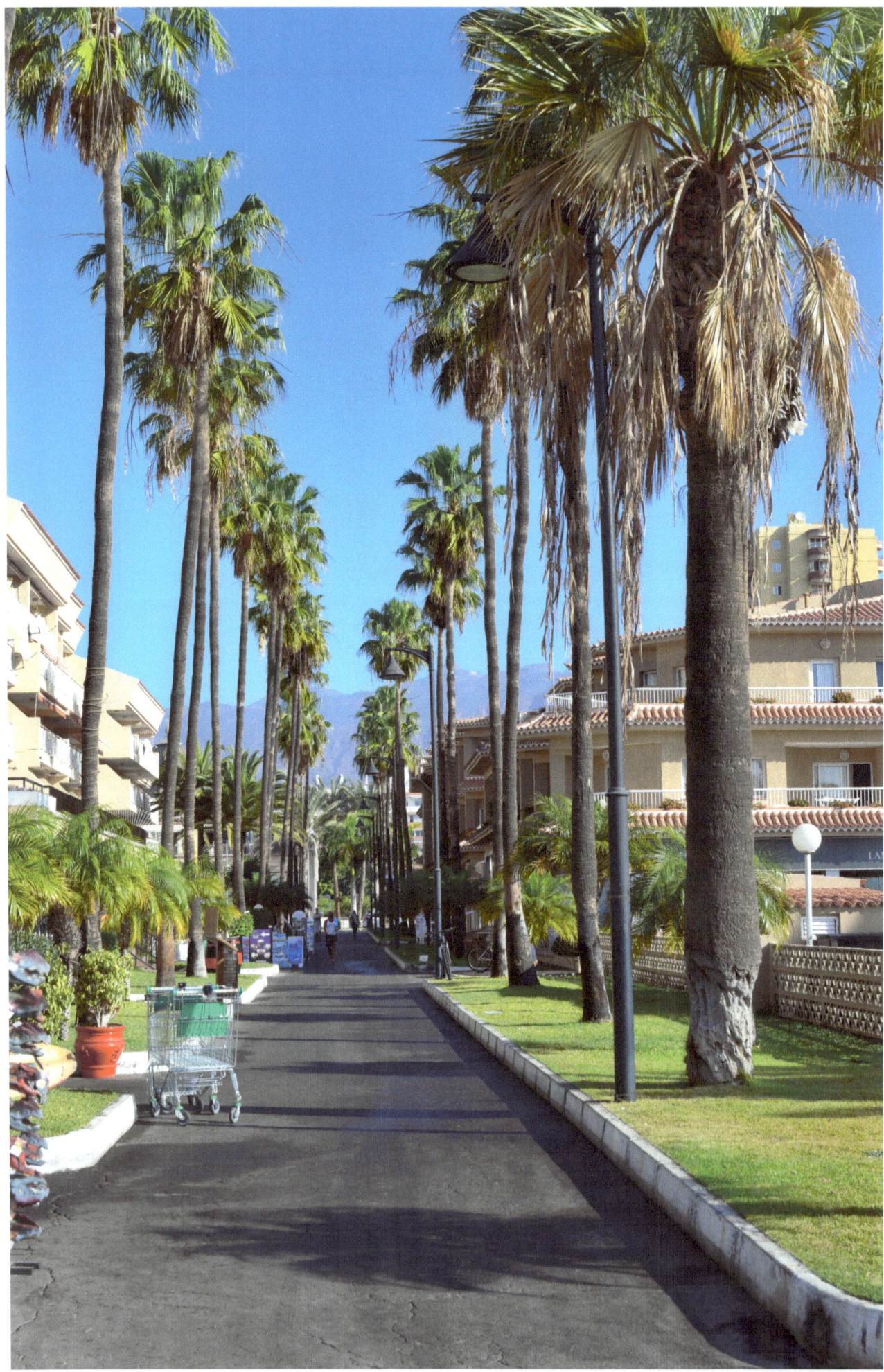

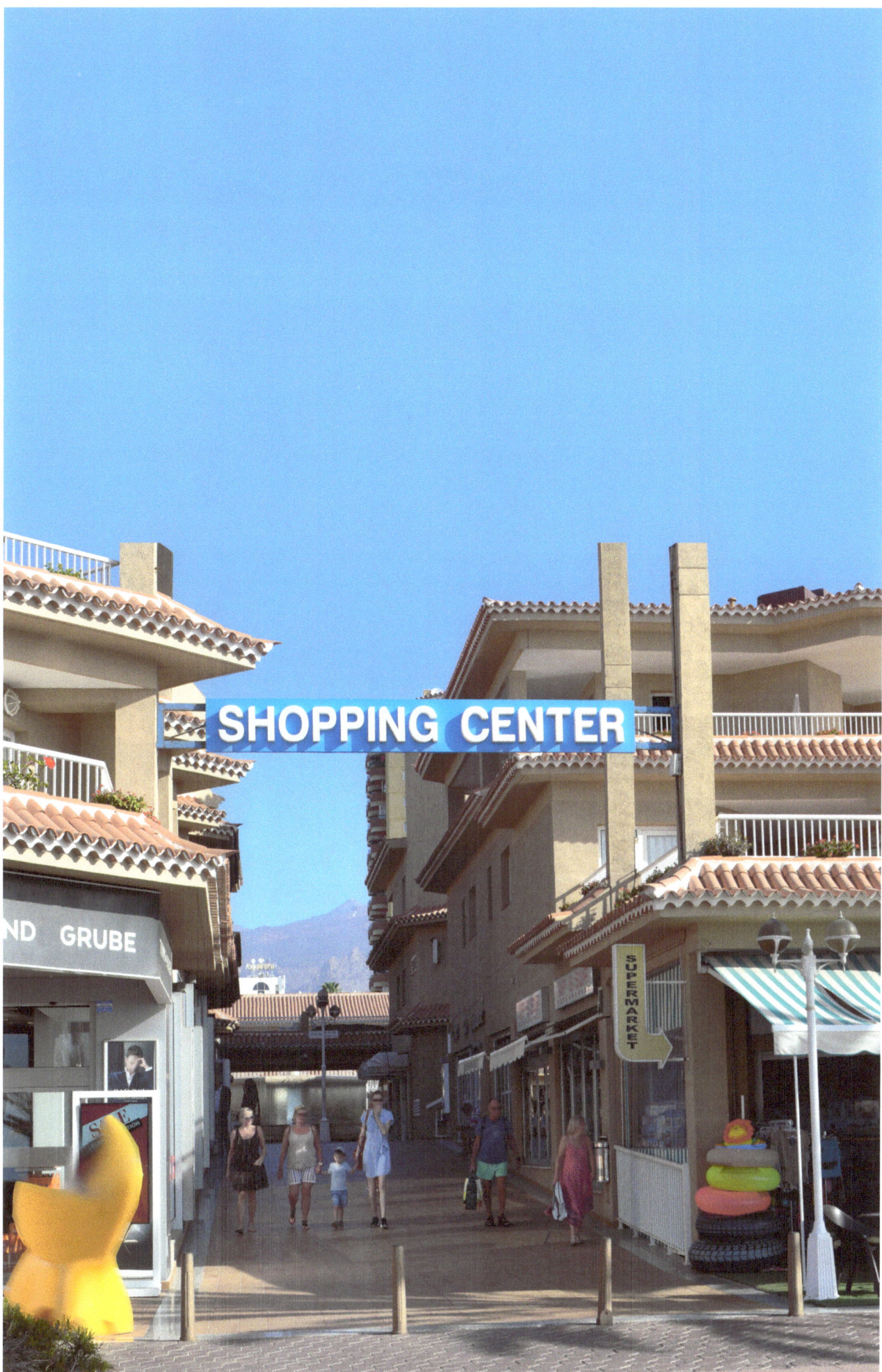

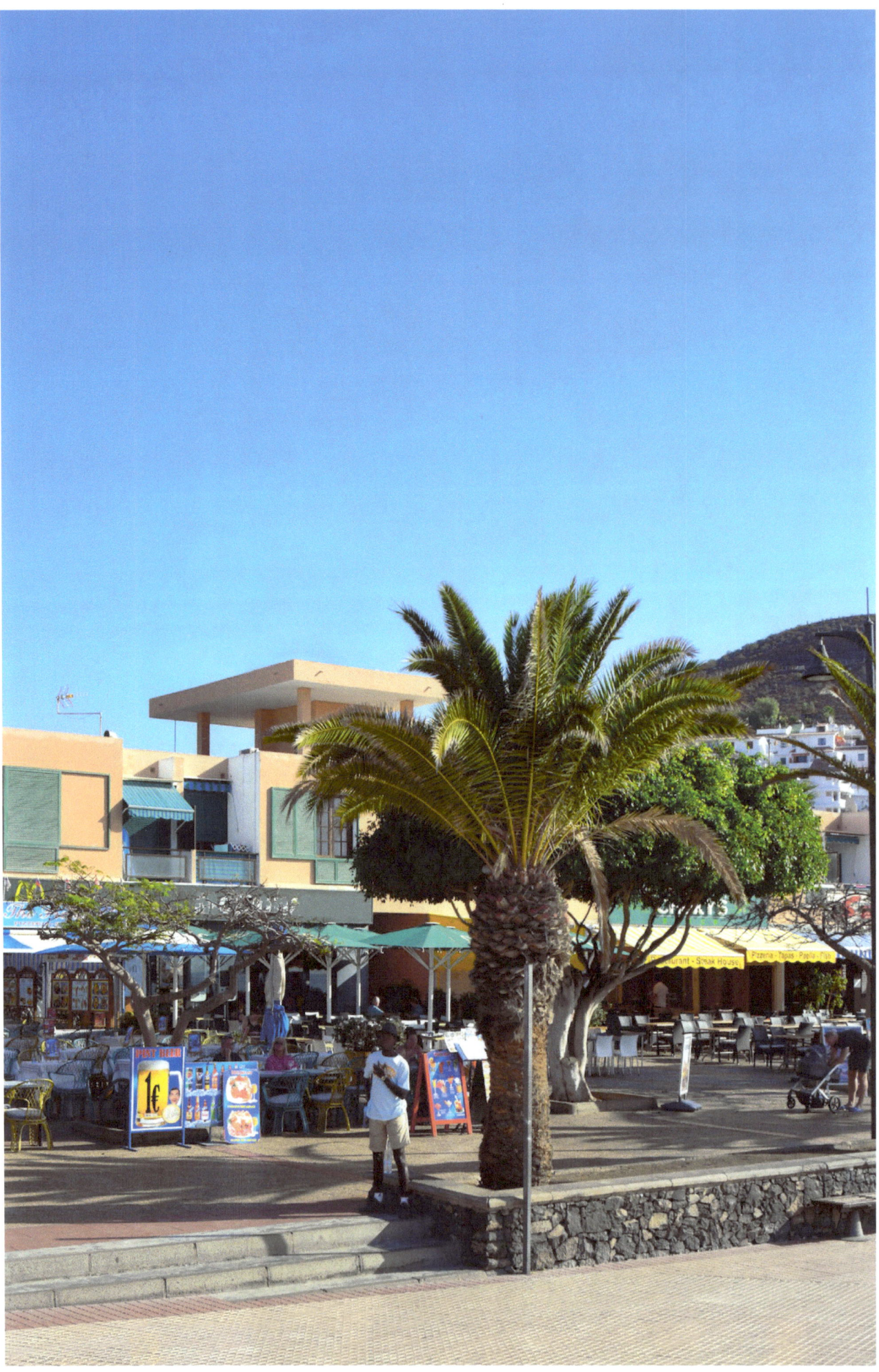

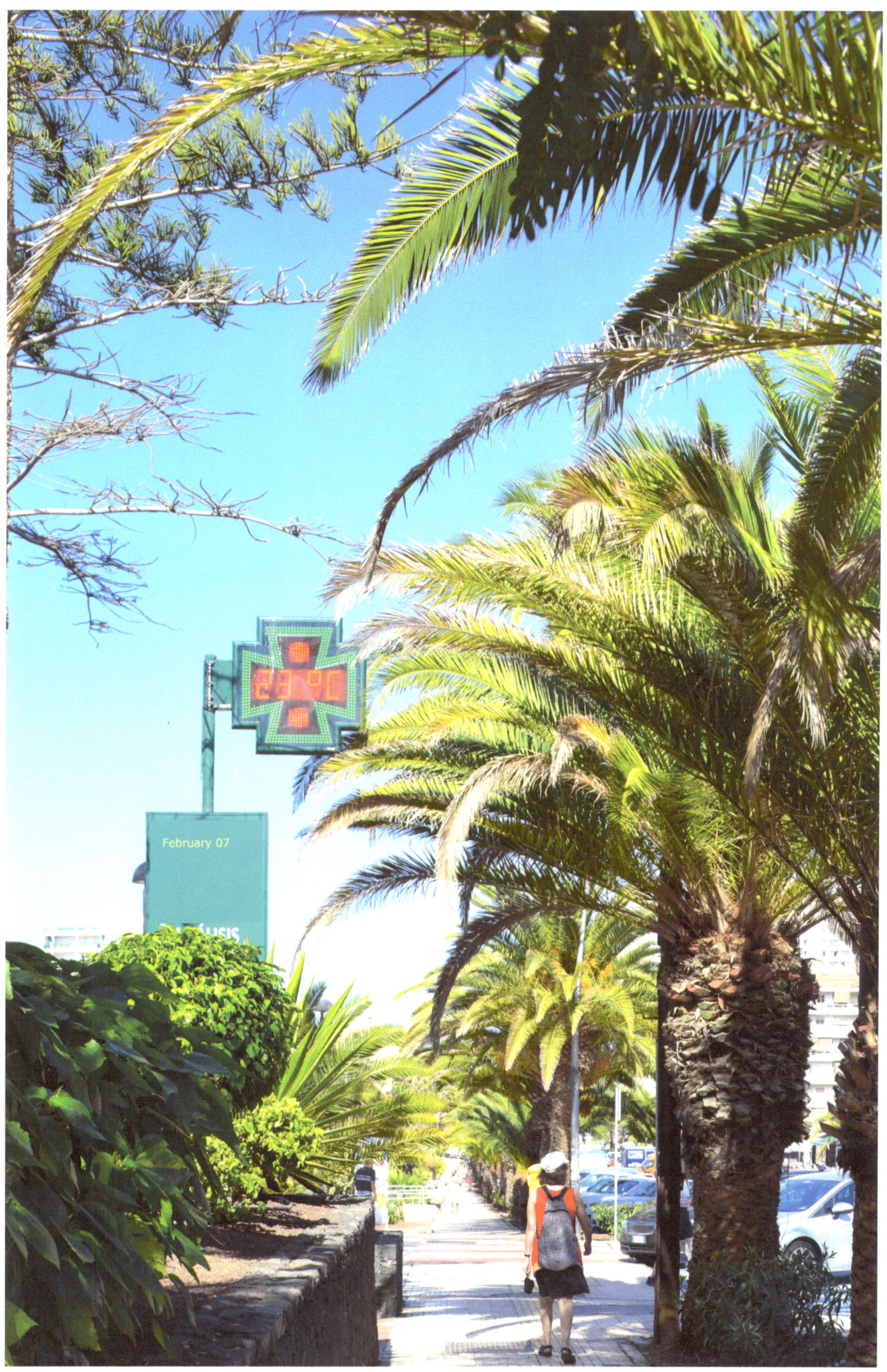

Global soft drink business brand. Coca-Cola brewed in the Canaries.

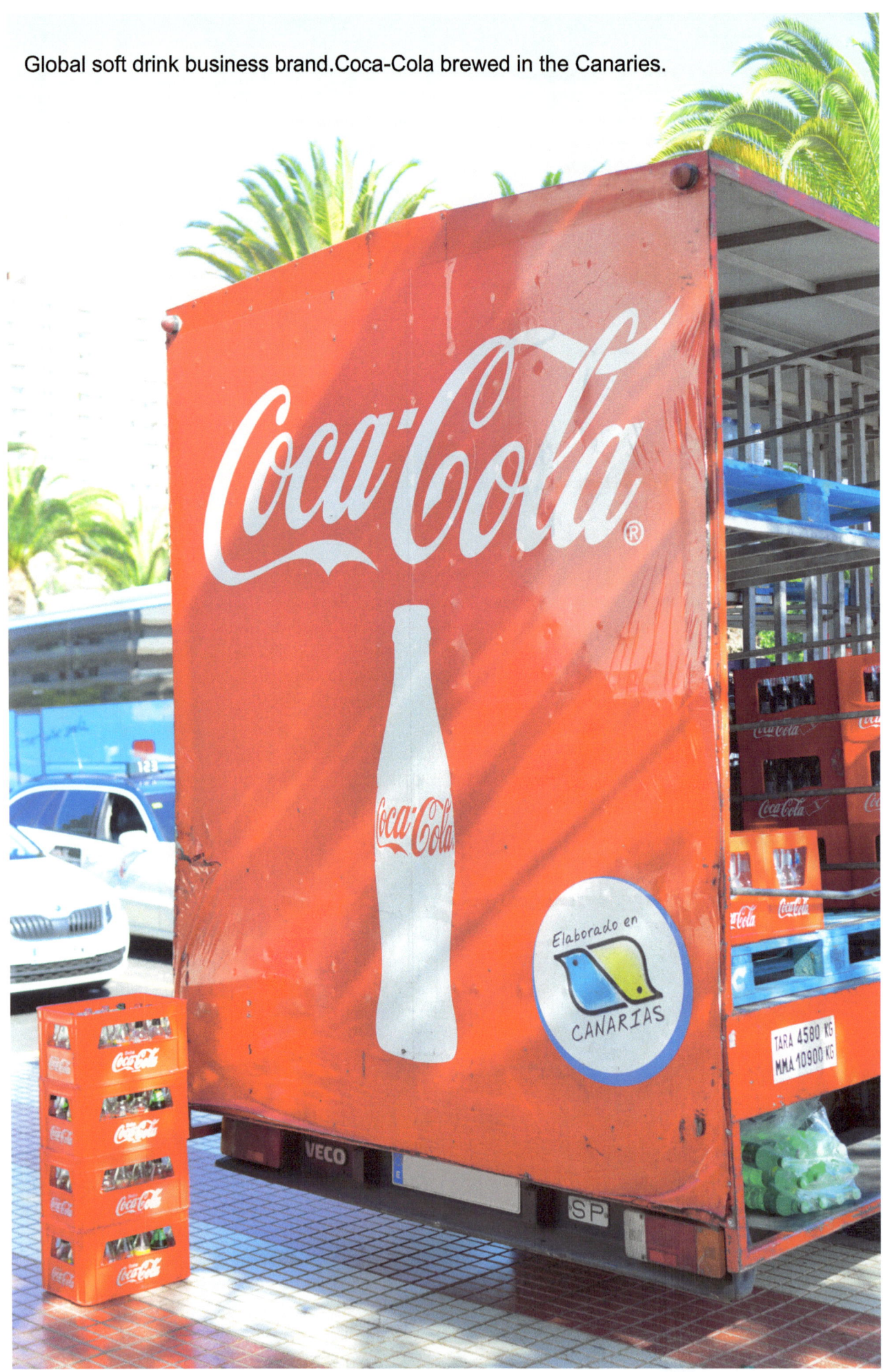

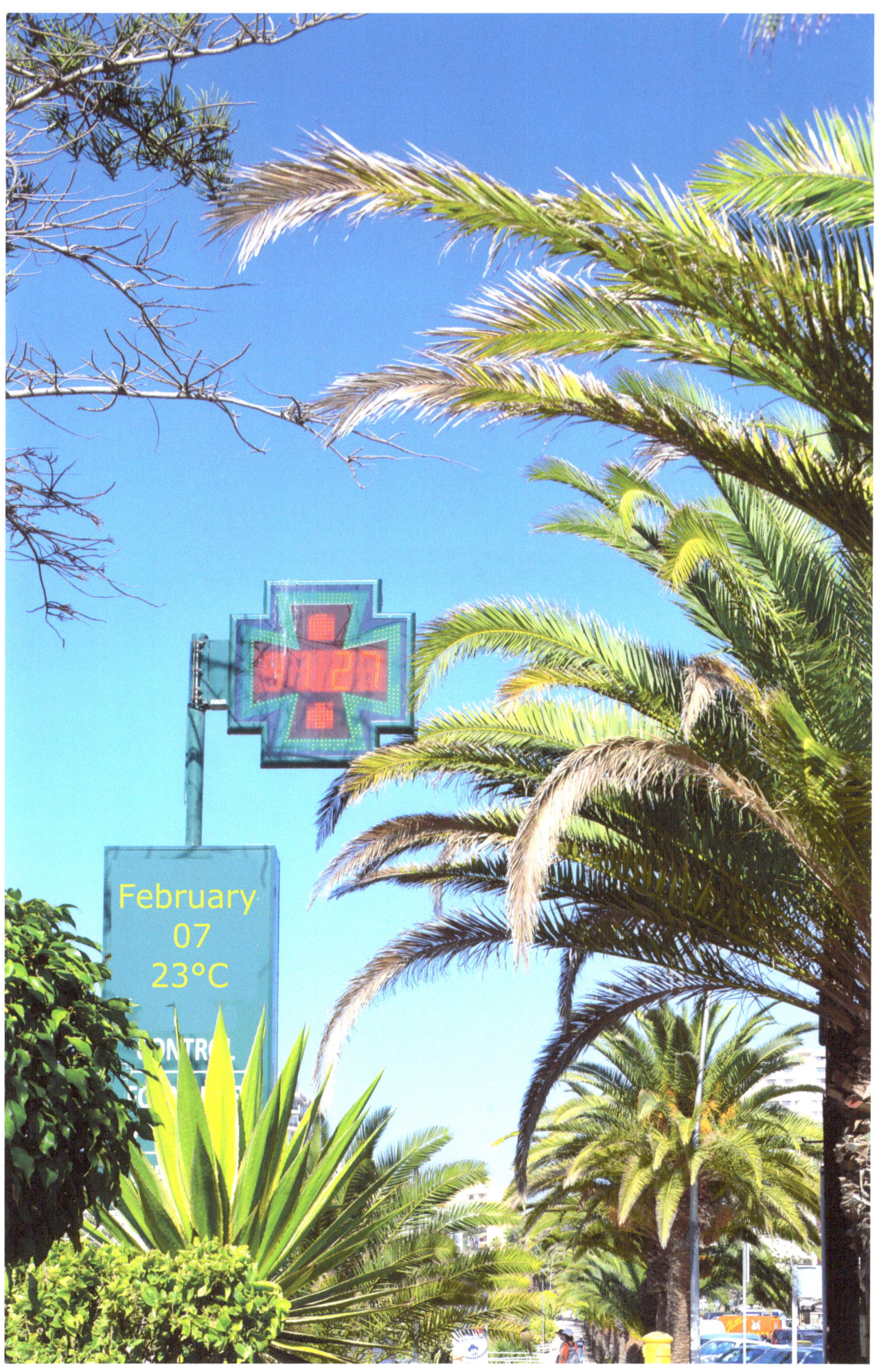

February
07
23°C

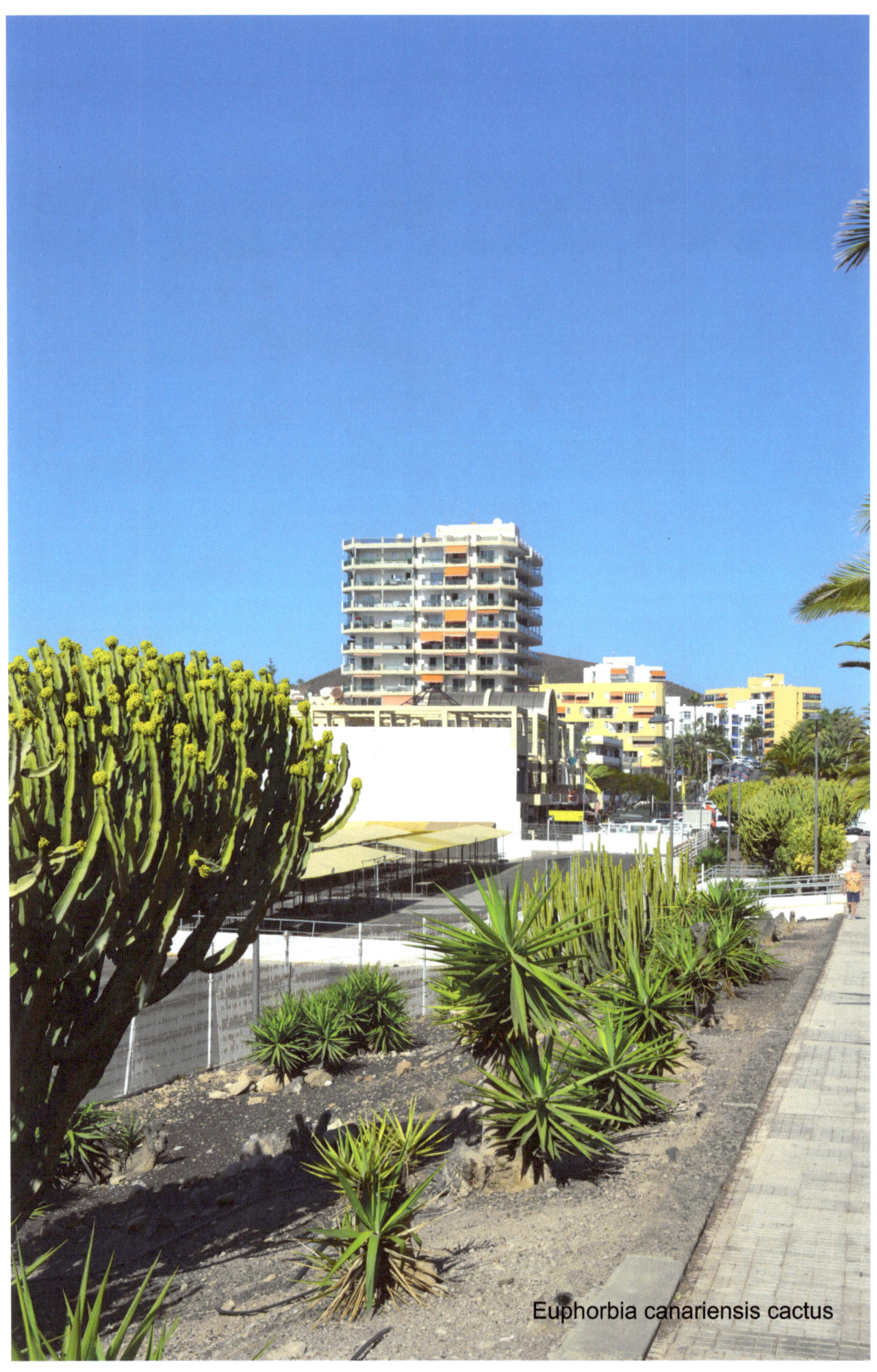
Euphorbia canariensis cactus

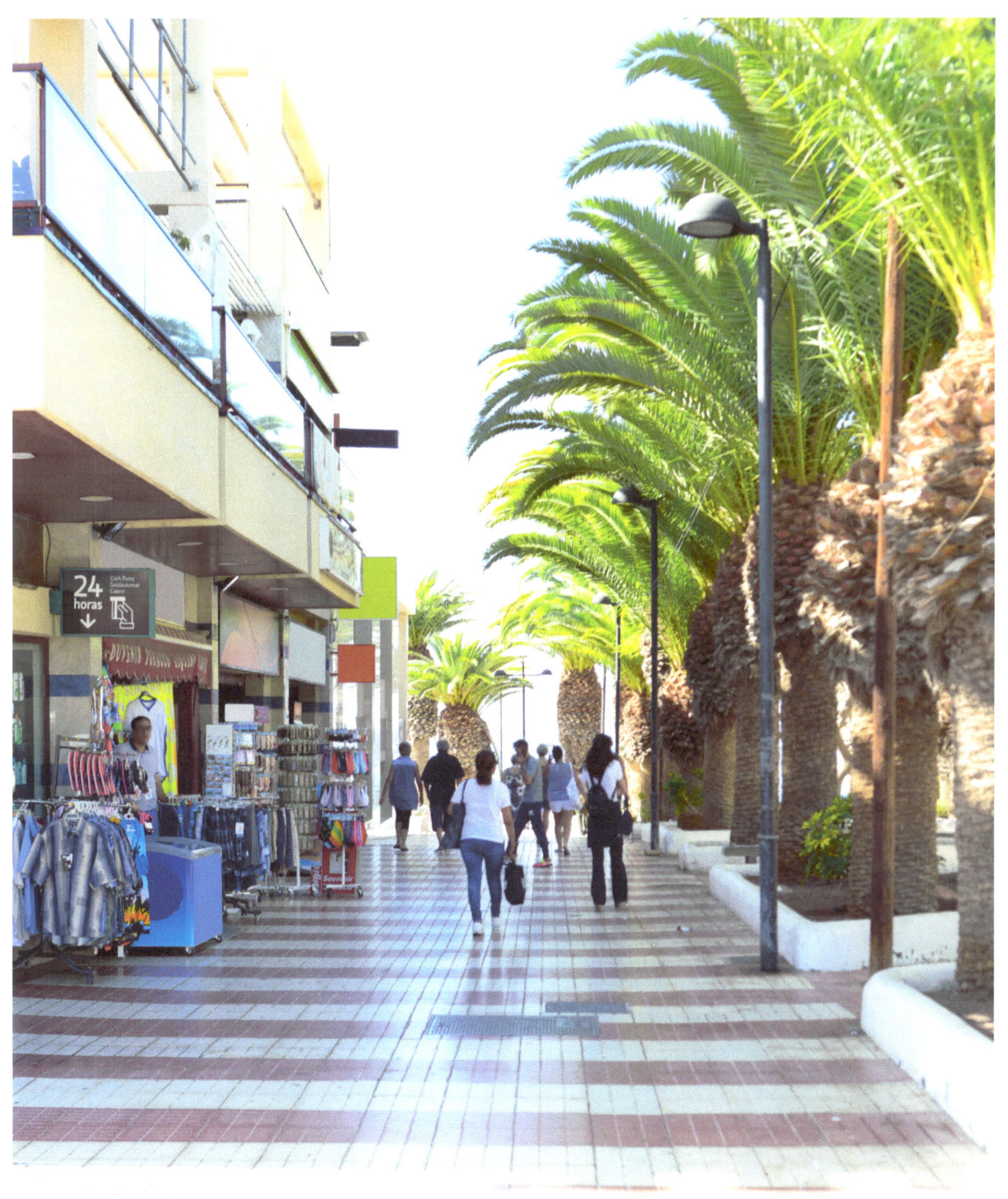

Playa de Las Américas, walking path to the beach.

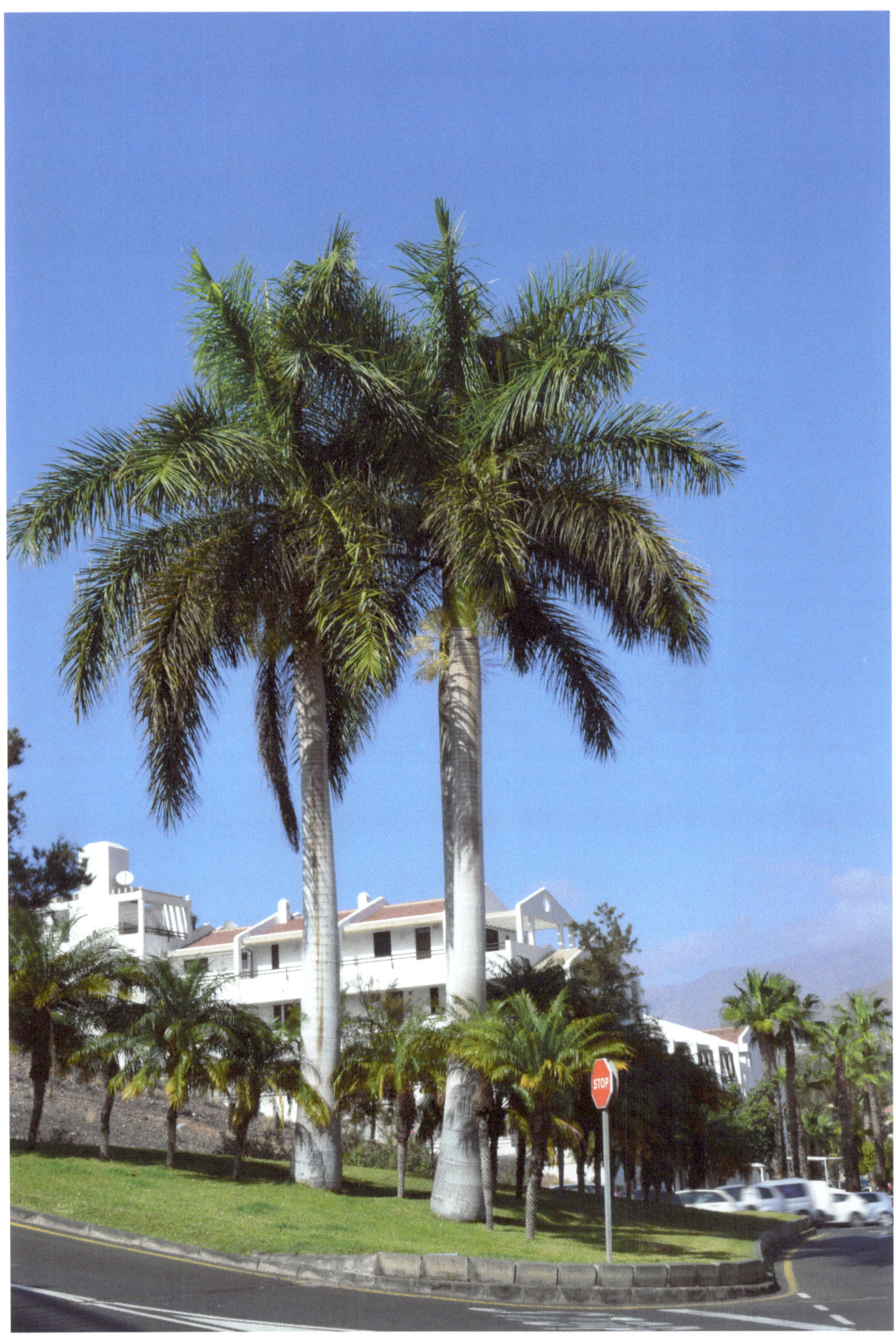

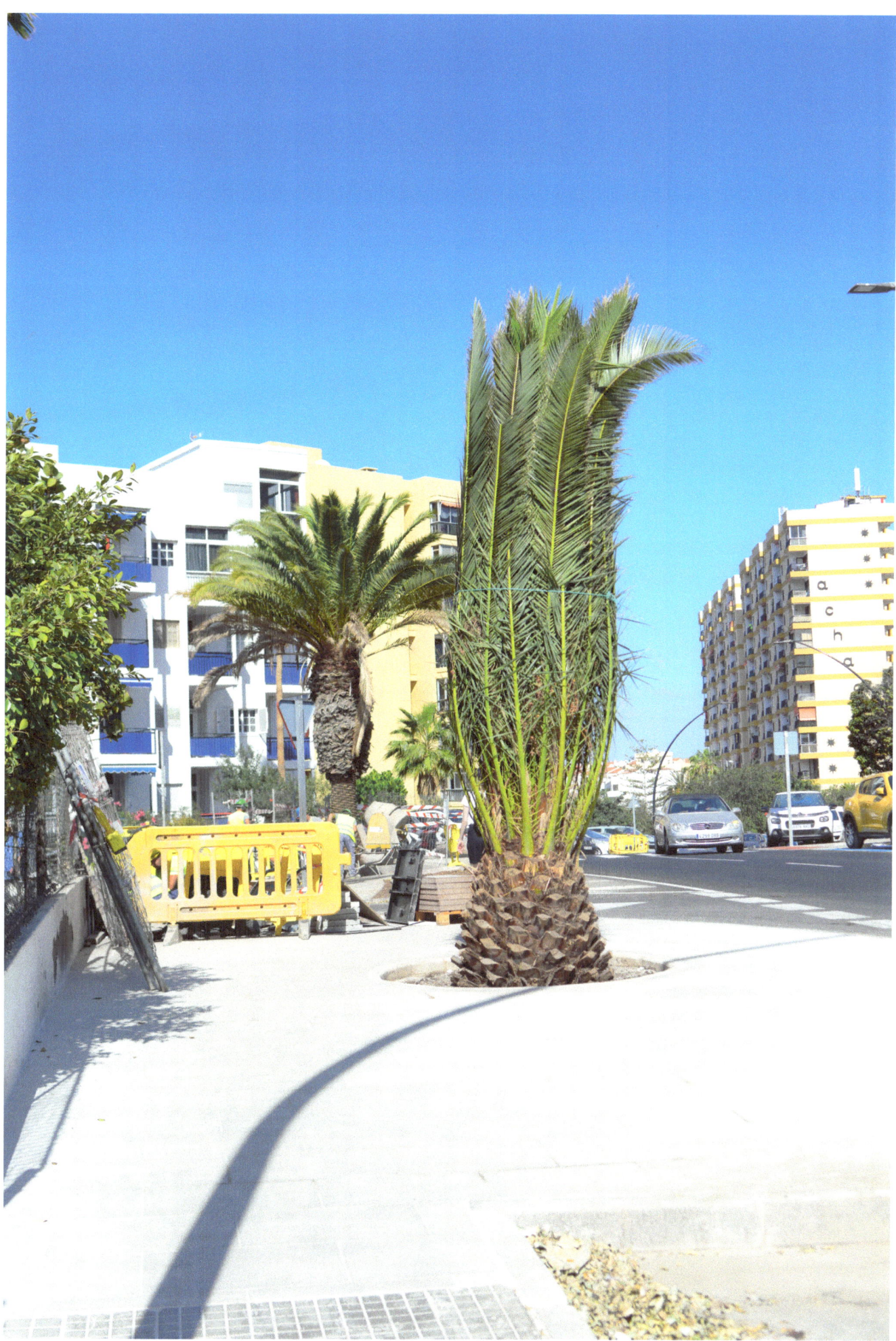

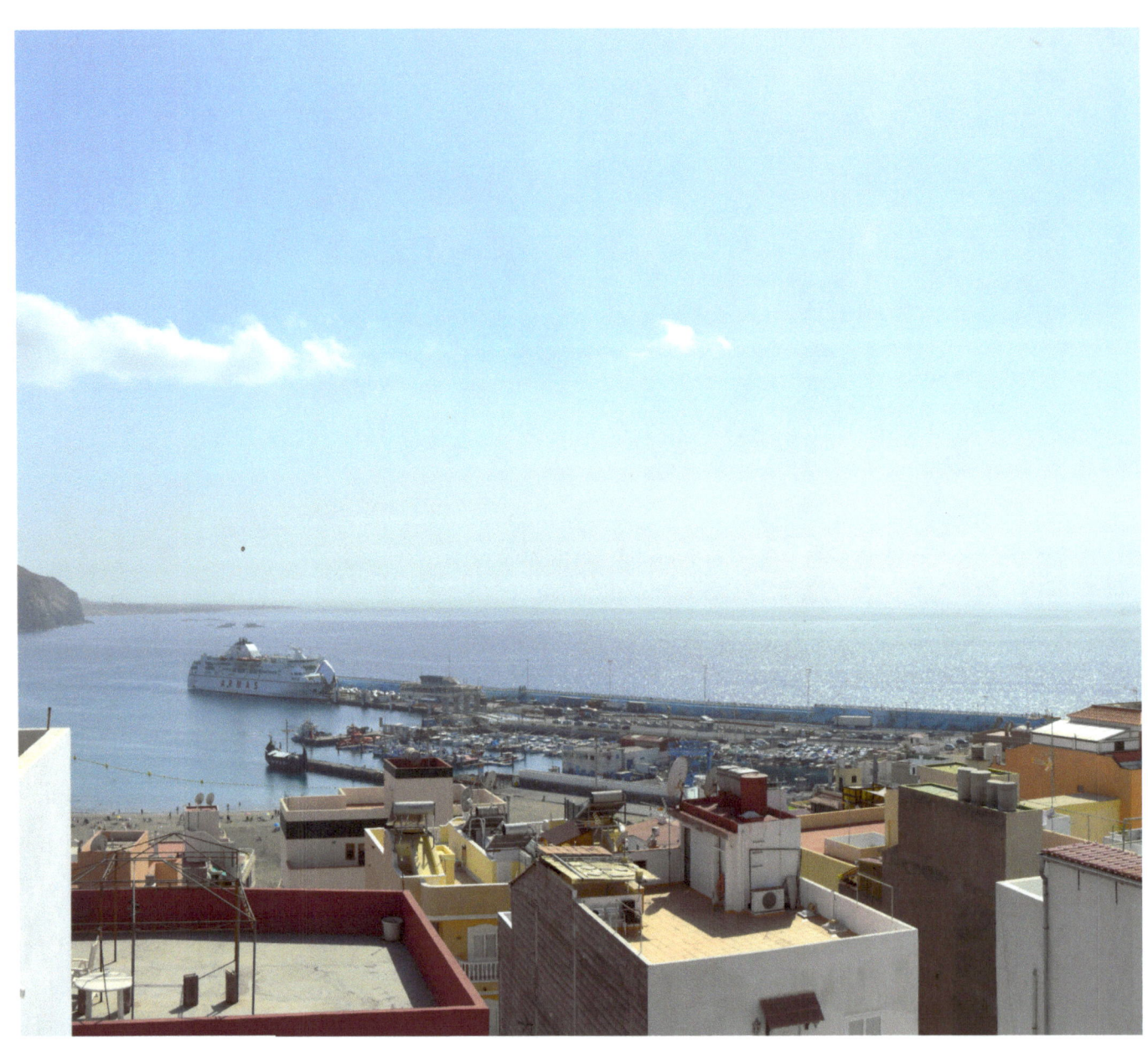

Port Los Cristianos, Arona, Santa Cruz de Tenerife.

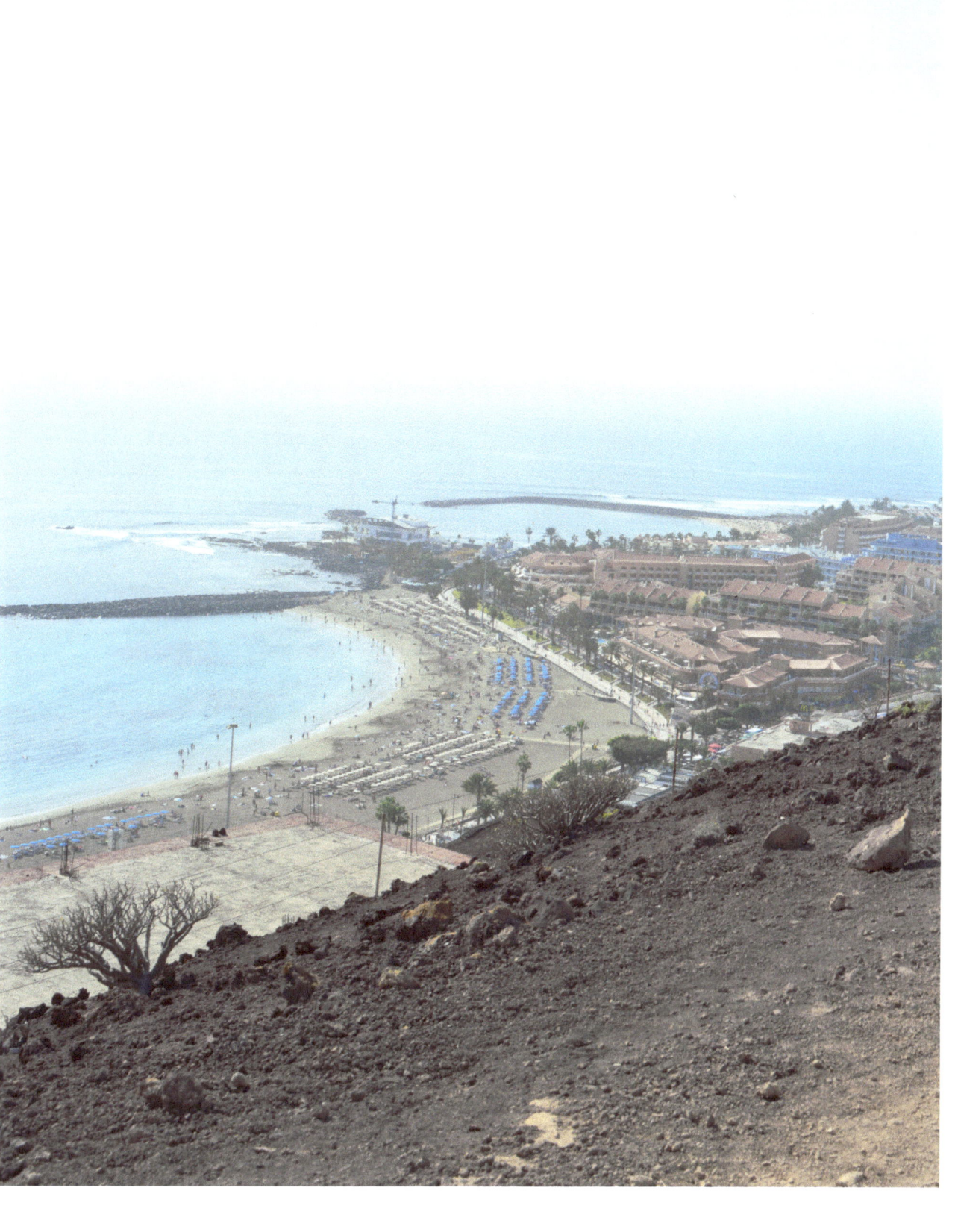

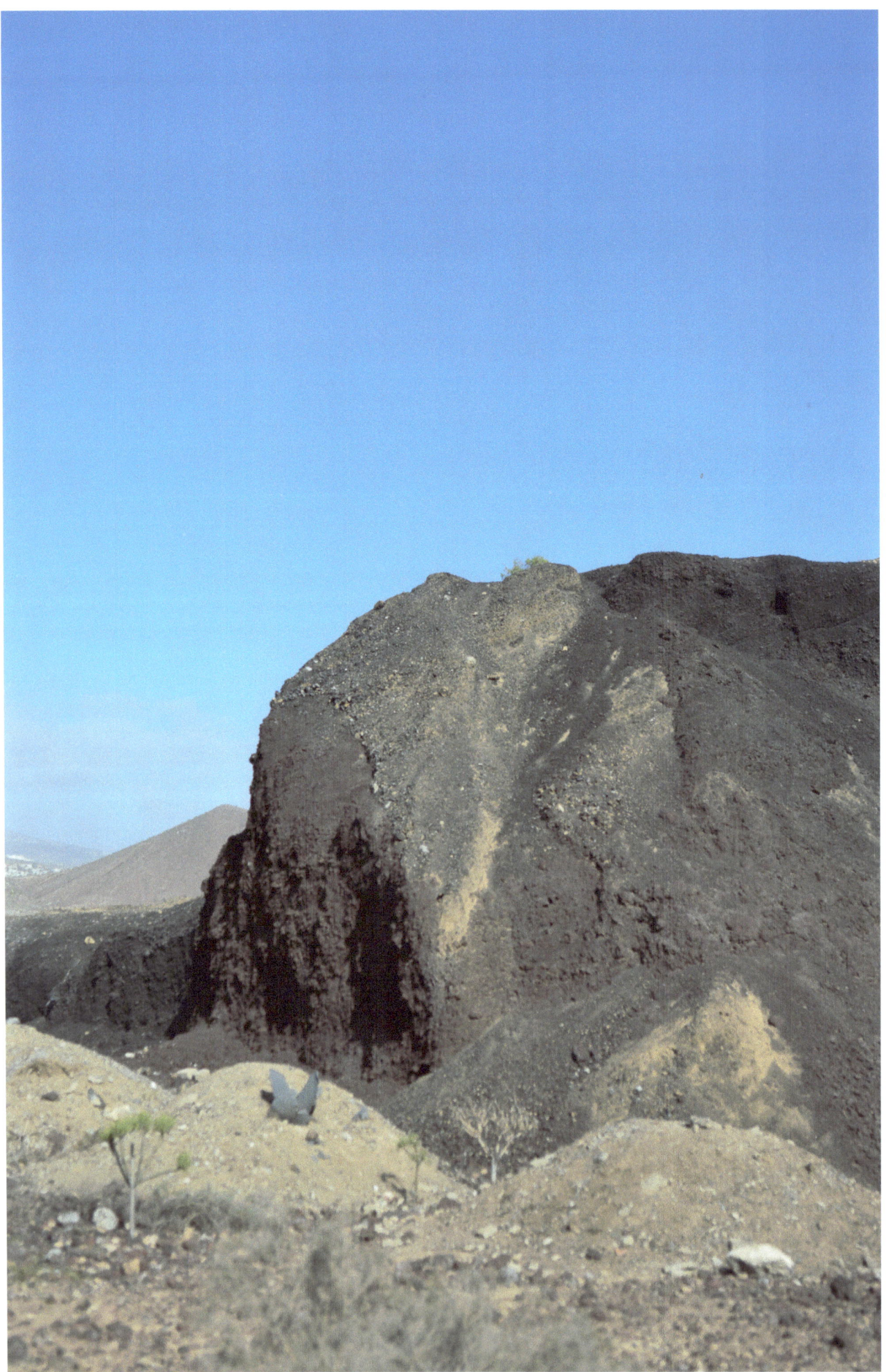

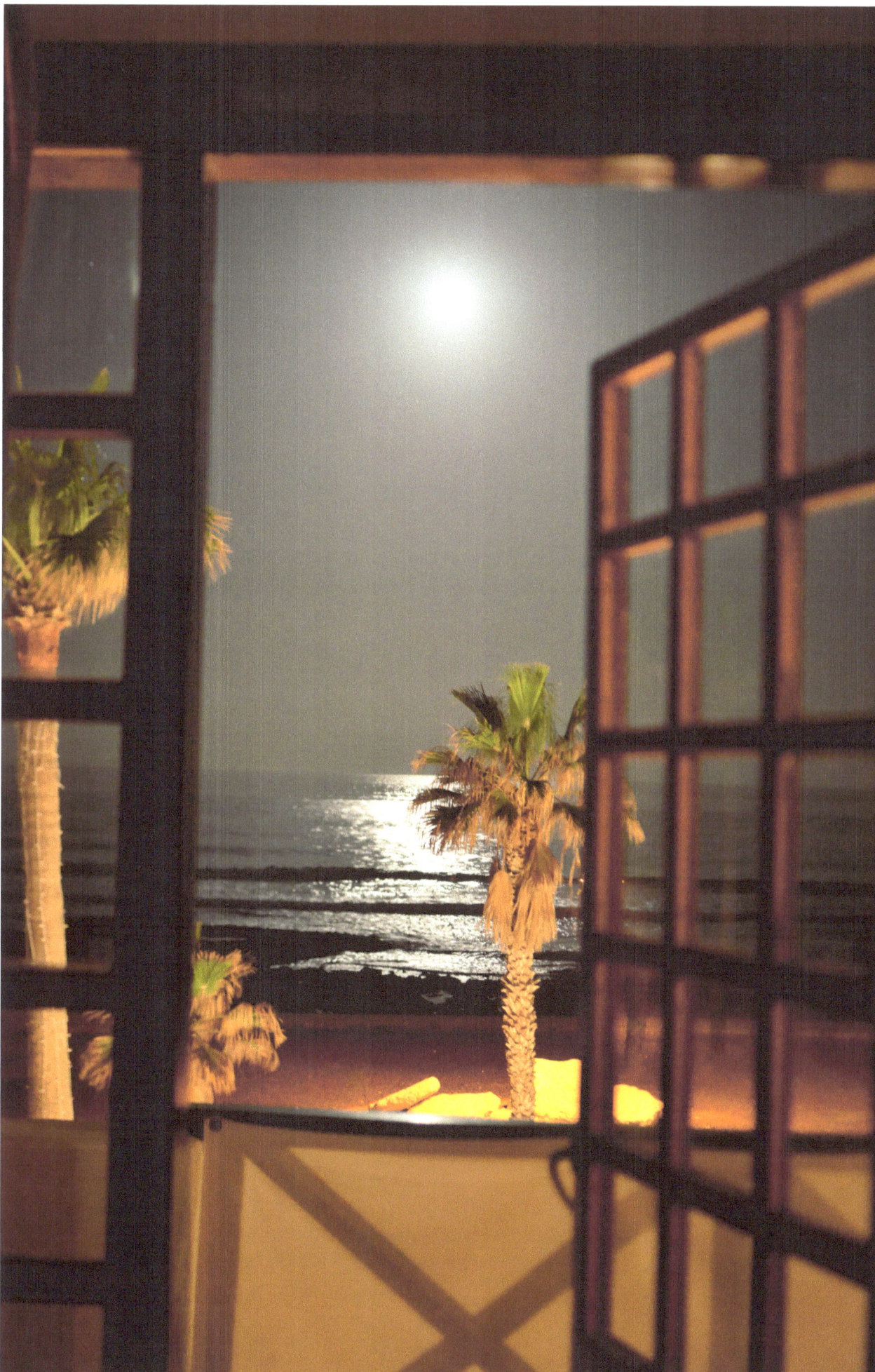

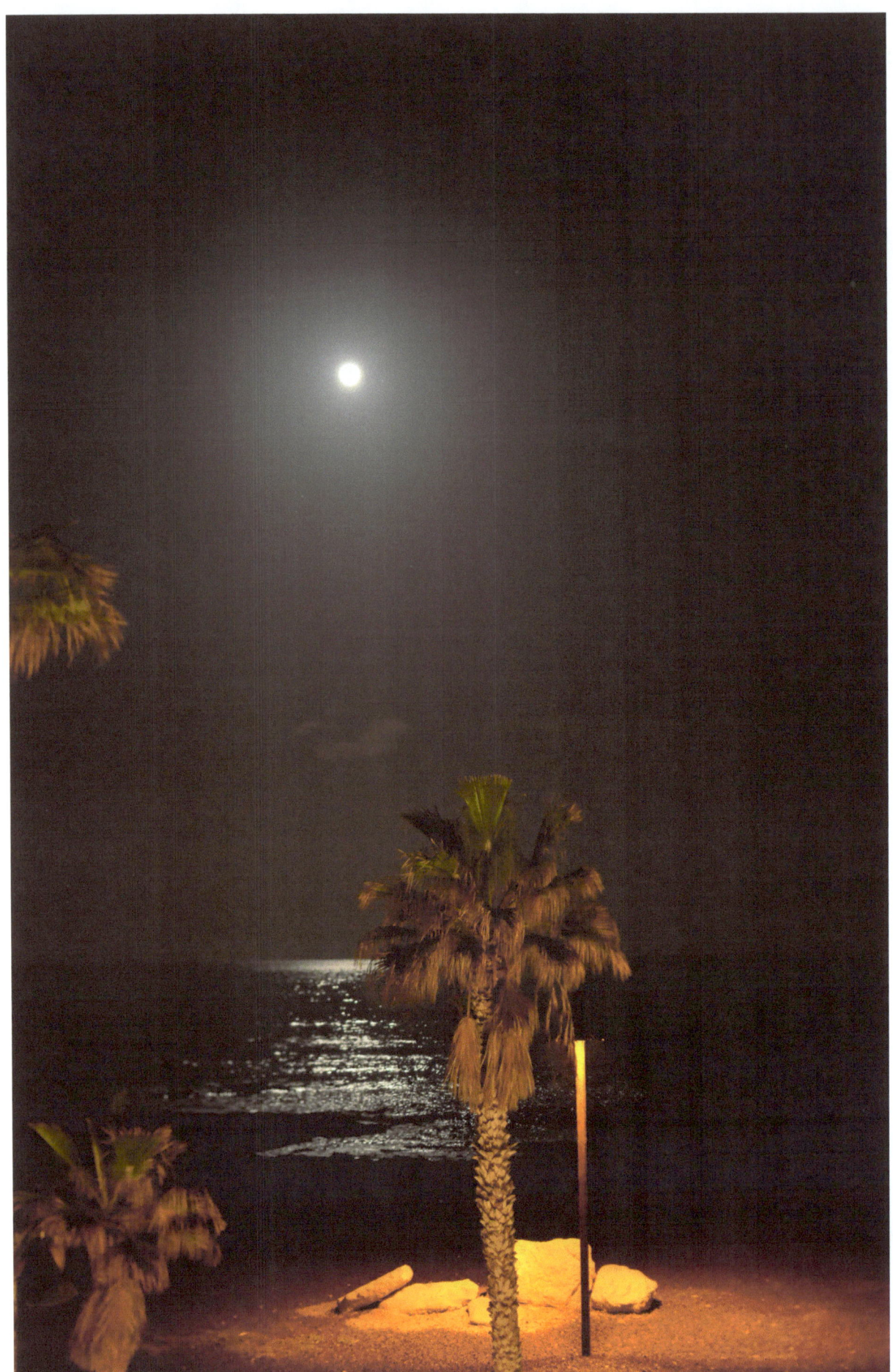